Patchwork

Shape

Written by Felicia Law
Illustrated by Paula Knight

Published by Mercury Junior

Painted squares

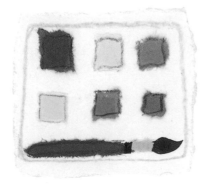

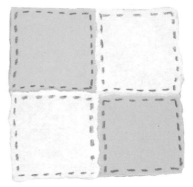

They are all there
On the squares
Of paper

My house
My Mum
My fingers
My thumbs

Triangle spangles

Three cheers for the queen

She sparkles and spangles

She glitters and glows

With shiny triangles

Her crown is a dazzle

Her robes bright and gay

Hang out the flags

For the queen, hip hooray!

Balls of fruit

Oranges, apples,
Melons and grapes
Tangerines, peaches,
All the same shape

Grapefruits and plums,
Fruits big and small
All tastes and colours
All round like a ball

Starfish

There are stars in the sky

But the ones that I like

Are down in the sea

With five pointed spikes

Musical tubes

Rum tum tum
Bang on the drum
Clickety click
Tap the pipe with a stick
Breathe deeply and blow
And the music will flow
With a peep and a piffle
From panpipe and whistle
Isn't it grand
The sound of our band!

Spinning circles

Round and round
Spins the big wheel so high
Carrying its passengers
Up to the sky
Round and round
Spin the wheels on my bike
As I ride to the park
To play 'catch' with Spike

Mountain tips

Up and up
The steep side of the mountain
Pulling our sledge as we go
Up and up
To the top of the mountain
Its tip all shiny with snow
Up and up
The slope gets steeper
Till we get to the top at last
Then sitting astride
The sledge, we ride
Sliding downhill very fast

Stripes

I ride a zebra

with stripes

on its nose

Up and down and roundabout the zebra goes

I ride a tiger

with stripes

on its coat

Up and down and roundabout the tiger floats

Semi circle

A great big slice of melon

Is wider than my mouth

So when I bite into it

The juice all dribbles out

Who's in the box?

Where is Timmy?
Where has he gone?
He's not in the box
I'm standing on

Where can he be?
Where can he hide?
Under the box?
No!
He's hiding inside!

This book introduces key words to your child

- apple
- ball
- box
- circle

- crown
- drum
- finger
- fruit

- grape
- house
- melon
- mountain

- mouth
- orange
- paper
- peach
- pipe
- plum
- round
- sledge
- snow
- square
- star
- starfish
- stripe
- tiger
- triangle
- tube
- wheel
- zebra

Mercury Junior
20 BLOOMSBURY STREET
LONDON WC1B 3JH

This edition published 2005 by
Mercury Books
20 Bloomsbury Street
London WC1B 3JH
ISBN 1-904668-85-2
Copyright © 2003 Allegra Publishing Ltd

Printed by D 2 Print Singapore